Monographic Journals of the Near East *Afroasiatic Linguistics* 5/6 (December 1978)

SEMANTIC PARAMETERS IN ANGAS KINSHIP TERMINOLOGY

by

Donald A. Burquest
Summer Institute of Linguistics
and
University of Texas at Arlington

This paper has two purposes: first, to present the facts of the system of kinship terminology of Angas; and second, to propose a formalism for representing such facts within linguistic descriptions. The analysis presented is purely formal, with no discussion of the cultural or functional expression of the system in behavior. A number of anthropological concepts are found to be useful in the description; of particular note are the principle of reciprocity, and the necessity of carrying out kinship investigations from the point of view of both male and female Ego. It is argued that the proposed formalism is superior to other such systems which have been proposed because of its capacity for ready integration into current linguistic theory because of format and rule type. A few concluding remarks are made regarding suggested application of the proposed formalism to matters of semantic change and reconstruction.

CONTENTS

0. INTRODUCTION

The term "Angas" is applied to an ethnic group of approximately 130,000[1] living in Pankshin Division, in the Plateau State of northern Nigeria. The term is apparently a corruption of the Angas term [ᵑgâs], which refers to the traditional characteristic tribal marking of a single scar down each cheek from temple to chin. The people involved do in fact use the term to refer to themselves, although the word [ᵑkʰàřᵊŋ], roughly translatable as 'people', is increasingly coming into favor ([ᵑkʰàřᵊŋ] is in wide use with the sense 'family' and may in fact be the original name for the tribal grouping).

The group so defined is a social entity, not a purely linguistic one, and there is some doubt about the extent to which even a traditional social unity can be strongly affirmed (it is only in recent years, for example, that the concept of a paramount chief was introduced by colonial officials). In fact, some groups which are better known by other names, e.g. Tal and Cip, consider themselves to be Angas, at least for some purposes. These two particular groups show a close linguistic affinity to one another (and to the group traditionally known as "Angas"), but also included under the "Angas" label is the population of the village of Myet, which bears no apparent linguistic relationship to the others.

The data described in this paper are based upon the language spoken in the Kabwir area, commonly referred to as "Plain Angas.[2] Newman and Ma (1966) classify the language as being in the Plateau Cluster of the Plateau-Sahel Group of Chadic languages. Culturally, the people who speak this language are patrilineal and virilocal.

The account of Angas kinship terminology presented in this paper is formal, not functional. My major interest is lexical, and I propose to present an ethnolinguistic study of the structure of the Angas kinship system. I will not be discussing the outworking in the culture of the kinship roles defined in the lexicon, nor will I be discussing terms which refer to units of social structure.[3]

1. ANGAS KINSHIP TERMINOLOGY

The theoretical position assumed here is that a system of kinship terminology, like any other portion of the lexicon of a language, reflects an organization of the phenomena of existence into clusters of manageable size. With particular reference to kinship, the system of kinship terminology employed by a language organizes the universe of kinsmen into distinct groupings, giving each such group a name, which is the kinterm itself. Just as a language may use terms such as TREE, BUSH, GRASS, etc. to subdivide at one level of

---

[1]According to the Nigerian census of 1962. It seems likely that speakers of Cip and Tal mentioned below are included in this figure.

[2]That is, as opposed to the speech of those referred to as "Hill Angas". It should be pointed out that this paper covers only the kinsmen and relatives represented in Figures 1 and 2; inclusion of others may require revision of the analysis proposed here. I am grateful to Yebir Bewarang and Nazhwak Gonap, who patiently provided most of the information contained here. I am grateful also to Marv Mayers and Carol McKinney, who read an earlier version of this paper and made several helpful comments. Recent studies of Plain Angas include Burquest (1971, 1973) and Jungraithmayr (1963, 1964b).

[3]An introductory discussion of Angas social organization can be found in Mohr (1948).

specification what is known scientifically as the plant kingdom, so terms such as FATHER, MOTHER, BROTHER, etc. are used to organize the universe of kinsmen.[4] A summary statement of the development of such terminological groupings is found in Tyler (1969:6-7):

> ". . . we do not live in a world in which we discriminate among all the possible sensory stimuli in our environment, nor do we react to each stimulus as if it were totally new and foreign. In effect, we choose to ignore many of those perceptual differences which make each object unique. In large part, we do this by naming . . . . It is through naming and classification that the whole rich world of infinite variability shrinks to manageable size and becomes bearable. Our methods of classification are entirely arbitrary and subjective. There is nothing in the external world which demands that certain things go together and others do not. It is our perception of similarities and differences together with a set of hierarchical cues that determine which things go together. We not only react to certain discriminable stimuli as if they were the same, we name them and organize them into groupings."

The chart in Figure 1 represents the system of Angas terms used to refer to the kinsmen and affines indicated, from the point of view of Ego as male. The terms given here are terms of reference, although most of them are used as terms of address as well. A few observations can be made by way of introduction:

(1) At the generation level two generations older than Ego (abbreviated here as G2), two terms appear: *kəka* and *gəzhet*. *Kəka* is used to refer to the mother of Ego's parents, as well as to her sisters and wives of her brothers, and to the sisters of the father of Ego's parents and his wives and the wives of his brothers. The terms used at G2 are applied to all more distant generations in the same way as well. We may gloss *kəka* as meaning 'grandmother', although as is true of all the glosses I will propose, the reference of the term is not the same as that of the English gloss. *Gəzhet* is used identically to refer to the comparable male kinsmen and affines. It may be glossed as 'grandfather' in the same fashion. Note that the terms are the same for parents of both male and female parents of Ego.

(2) At the generation level of Ego's parents (here abbreviated as G1), three terms appear: *pup*, *nən*, and *kən*. *Pup* is used to refer to Ego's father, his father's brothers, husbands of his father's sisters, and the husbands of the sisters of his mothers; it may be glossed as 'father'. The term *nən* is used similarly to refer to Ego's mother, her sisters, wives of her brothers, sisters of his father, and wives of brothers of his father; it may be glossed as 'mother'. The term *kən* is used at this generation level to refer solely to the brother of Ego's mother; it may be glossed as 'uncle'. Note that it is not used to refer to any kinsmen of Ego's father.

---

[4]Some scholars have argued that the system of kinship terminology employed by the speakers of a language tends to a large degree to reflect the patterns of social behavior manifested by them as well, e.g. Radcliffe-Brown and Forde (1950:9ff), Murdock (1949:107ff). That is, by classifying a group of kinsmen under a single term, the speaker to at least some extent equates them and thus relates to them behaviorally in the same manner. Murdock points out, however, that the match is not complete, and that such a hypothesis regarding correspondence between unity of terminology and unity of behavior must be approached with care (1949:108ff). As I noted above, the study of kinship behavior is outside the scope of this paper.

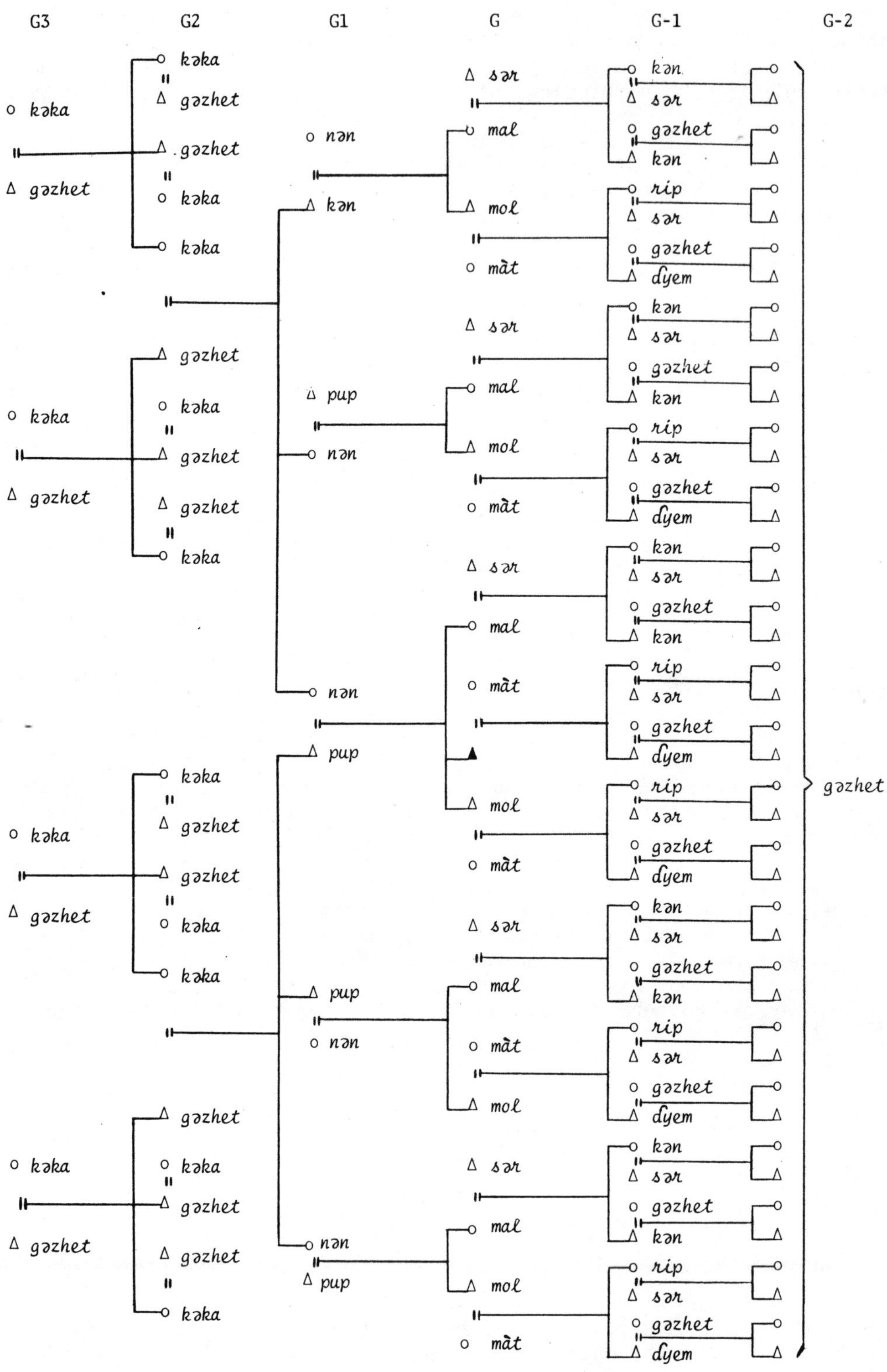

Figure 1. Angas Kinterms (Male Ego)

(3) At the generational level of Ego himself (abbreviated here as G), the following terms occur: *sər, mol, mal, màt*. *Mol* is used to refer to Ego's blood-brothers, as well as all male cousins (whether cross-cousins or parallel cousins); it may be glossed as 'brother'. *Mal* is used in an identical fashion to refer to Ego's blood-sisters, as well as all female cousins; it may be glossed as 'sister'. *Sər* and *màt* are both affinal terms and thus not strictly included in the system of kinship terminology.[5] However, in that some terms occur both as kinship terms and affinal terms, viz. *gəzhet, kəka, pup, nən*, I have included them in the discussion lest potentially important information be missed. *Sər* refers to the husband of anyone referred to as *mal* 'sister' (and it is generally used to refer to all in-laws) and may be glossed as 'in-law'. *Màt* refers to Ego's wife and the wives of anyone referred to as *mol* 'brother' (in its non-possessed form with high tone it is used generally to mean simply 'woman'), and it may be glossed as 'wife'.[6]

(4) At the generation level of Ego's children (here abbreviated as G-1), the following terms occur: *ɗyem, rip, kən, sər*, and *gəzhet*. The term *rip* refers to Ego's daughter, and the daughter of anyone referred to as *mol* 'brother'. It may be glossed as 'daughter'. The term *ɗyem* refers to Ego's son, and the son of anyone referred to as *mol* 'brother'. At a higher level of specification it is used more widely to mean 'child', thus including the kinsmen covered by the term *rip* 'daughter', and this use is common.[7] At the level at which it occurs in contrast with *rip*, however, it refers only to male descendants. We may thus gloss *ɗyem* as meaning 'son'. The term *kən* is the same as that used at generation level G1 to refer to Ego's mother's brother, but at this generation level it is used to refer to the offspring (both male and female) of anyone referred to as *mal* 'sister'. Although somewhat incongruous at this generation level, the gloss 'uncle', is still appropriate for reasons to be discussed below. The terms *sər* and *gəzhet* at this level are affinal terms, *sər* referring to the husband of anyone referred to as *kən* 'uncle' or *rip* 'daughter', *gəzhet* referring to the wife of anyone referred to as *kən* 'uncle' or *ɗyem* 'son'. The glosses 'in-law' and 'grandfather' may still be used (see discussion below).

(5) At the generation level of the children of Ego's children (abbreviated here as G-2), only the term *gəzhet* 'grandfather' occurs. It is used to refer to all offspring (both male and female) of anyone referred to as *ɗyem* 'son', *rip* 'daughter', or *kən* 'uncle' (the last being restricted in this sense to its use as a term at the G-1 level). The term *gəzhet furm* 'knee-grandfather' is optionally used at this level (and in more distant descending generations) to refer to the offspring of anyone referred to as *gəzhet* 'grandfather'. This may be considered to be an optional further specification of the term *gəzhet*, and as such it need not concern us further here.

Figure 2 represents the system of Angas kinterms and affinal terms from the point of view of Ego as female. It will be noted that at the generation levels G2, G1, and G, the terms

---

[5]The term *jur* 'co-wife' is excluded completely from this study; it specifies a relationship between the wives of Ego, rather than between Ego himself and someone else and thus lies outside the subject discussed here.

[6]It should be pointed out that there is no distinction made in terminology between older and younger siblings. The distinction CAN be made, of course, just as a distinction can be made between 'father' and 'father's brother' if required. But in this case it is made by the addition of the adjective 'small' or 'grown' not inherently a part of the kinship system, and such adjectival modification does not occur linguistically bound to the stems *mol* and *mal*. Further, its use is optional, and the key to understanding any kinship system lies in examination of the terms which are used obligatorily; otherwise all systems would be essentially the same in that all kinsmen in any system may be differentiated by paraphrase or modification if the situation demands it.

[7]In fact, the expression *ɗyem mat* 'woman-child' may be used instead of *rip* for 'daughter'.

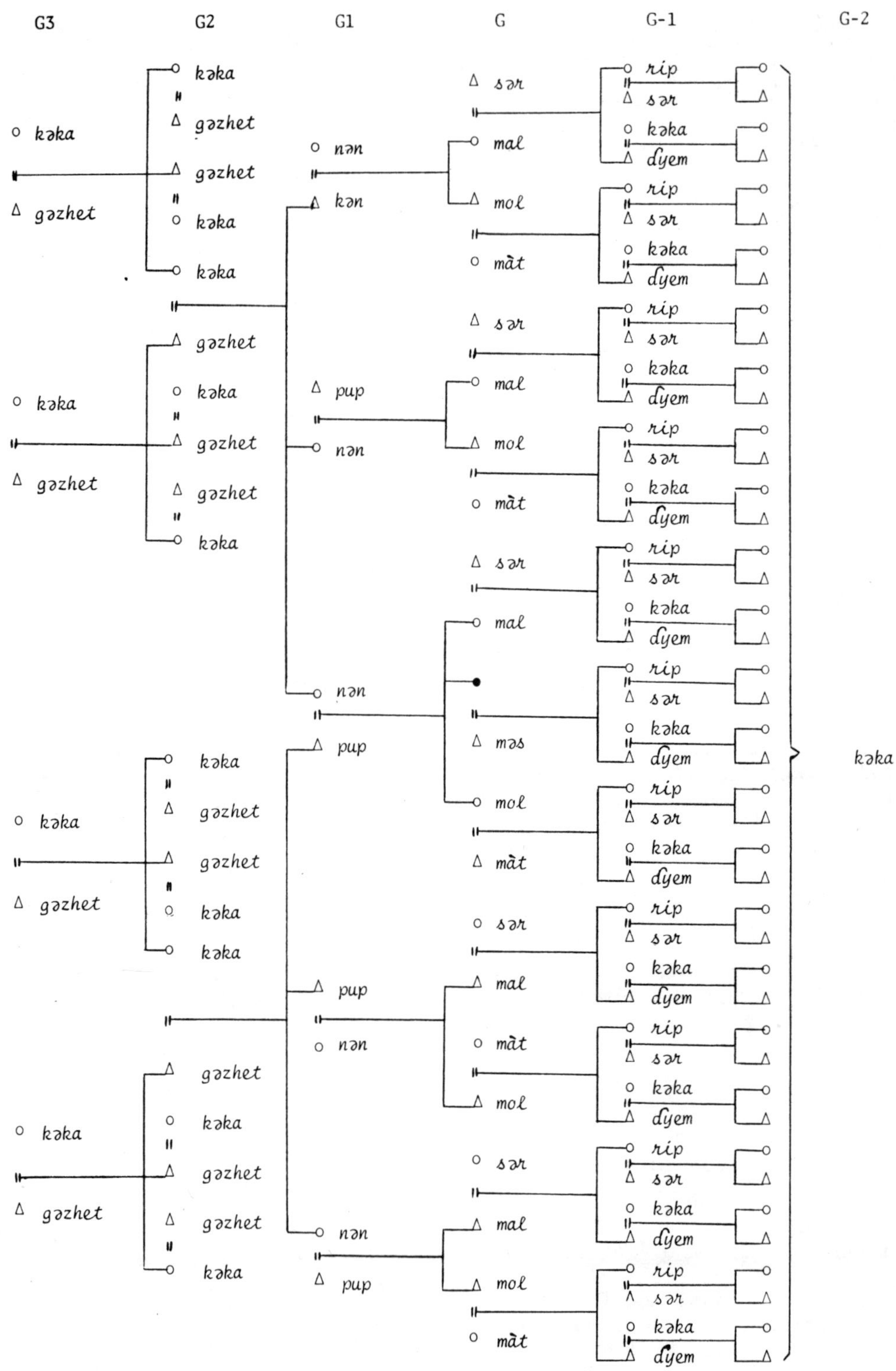

Figure 2. Angas Kinterms (Female Ego)

used in reference to relatives are the same as those employed when Ego is male, with the sole exception that Ego's mate is referred to as *məs* instead of *màt* 'wife'. We may gloss *məs* as meaning 'husband'.[8]

At generation levels G-1 and G-2, however, there are significant differences in terminology when Ego is female.

(1) At the generation level G-1 the only consanguineal terms which occur are *dyem* 'son' and *rip* 'daughter'. There are no instances of *kən* 'uncle' being used to refer to the offspring of Ego's *mal* 'sister', but *dyem* and *rip* are used instead. The same terms *dyem* and *rip* are used also to refer to the offspring of anyone referred to as *mol* 'brother', just as they are used from the point of view of male Ego. Also, the use of the term *sər* 'in-law' to refer to the husband of anyone referred to as *dyem* is the same as when Ego is male (except of course for the inapplicabliity of the specification of its use referring to the husband of anyone referred to as *kən* 'uncle', which was necessary in the former instance). But instead of *gəzhet* 'grandfather' which is used by male Ego, the term *kəka* 'grandmother' is used by female Ego to refer to the wife of anyone referred to as *dyem*.

(2) At the generation level G-2 the only term which occurs is *kəka* 'grandmother', used to refer to both male and female offspring of anyone referred to (in this case) as *dyem* 'son', thus paralleling the use of *gəzhet* 'grandfather' by male Ego. Further, the term *gəzhet furm* 'knee-grandfather' used by male Ego to refer to offspring of *gəzhet* is replaced in the case of female Ego by the expression *kəka furm* 'knee-grandmother' to refer to the offspring of *kəka*. As is true at the other end of the classification, these same terms which are used at generation level G-2 are used also at generation levels G-3 and beyond in the same way.[9]

---

[8]Note that female Ego has *məs* as an additional (rather than replacive) kinship term, because the term *màt* 'wife' is used also by female Ego to refer to the wife of anyone referred to as *mol* 'brother', just as was the case for male Ego. I return to this point below.

[9]In anthropological discussions of kinship systems as found in standard works, six major types are generally discussed: Eskimo, Iriquois, Hawaiian, Crow, Omaha, and Sudanese. Each type has characteristic features of kinship terminology at the G1 and G generational levels which are taken as being diagnostic of the type. The Angas system fails to be of the Eskimo type because it equates cousins with siblings, and (with the exception of MoBr) the siblings of Ego's mother and father with mother and father respectively according to sex.

In the Iriquois system parallel cousins are treated as equivalent to siblings, with cross-cousins treated separately; further, FaBr and MoSi are treated as the same as father and mother respectively, while FaSi and MoBr are treated separately (obviously utilizing the same principle as that for cousins). The Angas system fails to be of the Iriquois type because it equates ALL siblings of Ego's parents (with the exception of MoBr) with parents and in addition treats all cousins in the same way.

The Hawaiian system equates all cousins with siblings and all siblings of Ego's parents with the parents themselves. The Angas system fails to be of the Hawaiian type because of the sole occurrence of *kən* 'uncle' as MoBr instead of utilizing the same term as that for father which is characteristic of this type.

Angas fails to be of the Crow or Omaha type because it has no terms which apply to consanguineal kinsmen of both generation level G1 and G as each of these systems does.

The characteristic feature of the Sudanese kinship type is the specific terminology used to denote cousins, each particular one having its own specific term. In grouping all cousins together and equating them with brother and sister, Angas identifies itself as being not of the Sudanese type.

2. PRINCIPLES OF RELATIONSHIP EMPLOYED

In a very old work, Kroeber (1909:239-240) proposes eight major principles of relationship which can exist among kinsmen, characterizing them as principles of generation, collaterality, relative age within a generation, sex of the kinsman, sex of the speaker, sex of the person through whom the relation exists, consanguineality, and condition of life of the person through whom the relation exists. I have already pointed out that relative age within a generation is not relevant in the Angas system, and the condition of life of the person through whom the relation exists, e.g. if dead or divorced, does not appear to be relevant either. The principle of the sex of the person through whom the relation exists seems to distinguish MoBr (*kən*) from FaBr (*pup*), so it is applicable to at least that pair of terms. The other five principles are also applicable, and it will be useful to discuss the Angas terms in relation to them.

The classification of the terms according to the parameter of generation is shown in (1):[10]

(1)	Male Ego			Female Ego		
generation-restricted	*kəka*	'grandmother'	G2	*gəzhet*	'grandfather'	G2
	pup	'father'	G1	*pup*		G1
	nən	'mother'	G1	*nən*		G1
				kən	'uncle'	G1
	mol	'brother'	G	*mol*		G
	mal	'sister'	G	*mal*		G
	màt	'wife'	G	*màt*		G
				məs	'husband'	G
	dyem	'son'	G-1	*dyem*		G-1
	rip	'daughter'	G-1	*rip*		G-1
non-restricted	*gəzhet*	'grandfather'	G2, G-1, G-2	*kəka*	'grandmother'	G2, G-1, G-2
	kən	'uncle'	G1, G-1			
	sər	'in-law'	G, G-1	*sər*	'in-law'	G, G-1

So of the six major types of kinship systems discussed in the literature, Angas falls into none of the classifications, although it fails in only a single point to be of the Hawaiian type (at least for the generations which are generally accepted as being diagnostic). I do not mean to be suggesting that the Angas system is a new discovery, because it seems to be fairly common in Africa; but I have come across no discussion of such a system in the literature.

In classification by first ascending generation (abbreviated here as G1), Angas is clearly of the type known as Generational, in that that is the only type which identifies all consanguineal female kinsmen of G1 by the same term (such classification being the diagnostic feature for first ascending generation classification).

[10]The classification here is based upon the data in the charts only.

By the designations G2 and G-2 I mean to include all more distant generations in accordance with the preceding discussion. The terms *kəka* 'grandmother' and *gəzhet* 'grandfather' are grouped together on the chart to capture their equivalent usage by male and female Ego (I return to this discussion below). In light of the evidence in (1), we may conclude that to a large extent the concept of generation is operative in Angas terminology, although there are some terms to which it does not apply.

The principle of collaterality has to do with whether or not consanguineal kinsmen of the same generation and sex are referred to by the same term. When classified according to this criterion, Angas kinship and affinal terms fall into the groups presented in (2):

(2)

	Male Ego		Female Ego	
all males of G2	*gəzhet*	'grandfather'	*gəzhet*	
all females of G2	*kəka*	'grandmother'	*kəka*	
all females of G1	*nən*	'mother'	*nən*	
all males of G	*mol*	'brother'	*mol*	
all females of G	*mal*	'sister'	*mal*	
all males of G-1			*ɗyem*	'son'
all females of G-1			*rip*	'daughter'
all of G-2	*gəzhet*	'grandfather'	*kəka*	'grandmother'
non-restricted	*pup*	'father'	*pup*	
	kən		*kən*	
	ɗyem	'son'		
	rip	'daughter'		

The complicating factor here is that *kən* 'uncle' is used to refer to MoBr in G1, while *pup* 'father' refers to all other consanguineal males; and for male Ego at generation level G-1 both *kən* 'uncle' and *ɗyem* 'son' are used to refer to males, and both *kən* and *rip* 'daughter' are used to refer to females. In light of the data in (2), we may conclude that the criterion of collaterality is widely applicable in the Angas kinship system.

When classified according to the parameter of the sex of the kinsman involved, Angas kinship and affinal terms fall into the groups presented in (3):

(3)

	Male Ego		Female Ego	
restricted to male relatives	*pup*	'father'	*pup*	
	mol	'brother'	*mol*	
	sər	'in-law'	*sər*	
			gəzhet	'grandfather'
			kən	'uncle'
	ɗyem	'son'	*ɗyem*	

(3) cont.

restricted to female relatives	*nən*	'mother'	*nən*	
	mal	'sister'	*mal*	
	màt	'wife'	*màt*	
	rip	'daughter'	*rip*	
	kəka	'grandmother'		
non-restricted	*gəzhet*	'grandfather'	*kəka*	'grandmother'
	kən	'uncle'		
			məs	'husband'

In reality *sər* 'in-law' is not restricted to male affines (see below), but in terms of the chart data it is restricted, and it is this data which is presented in (3). The classification of *ɗyem* 'son' as being restricted to male kinsmen is in accordance with earlier discussion regarding its use as specifying kinsmen of both sexes in that in the latter usage it is employed at a higher level of specification. The use of *məs* 'husband' as referring to relatives of both sexes when used by female Ego will be discussed below. Again, the criterion is widely applicable, and the exceptions require explanation (I return to this matter below).

The criterion of the sex of the speaker is relevant only for the terms presented in (4):

(4)	Male Ego		Female Ego	
child of *mal*	*kən*	'uncle'	*ɗyem*	'son'
			rip	'daughter'
wife of child of *mal* or *mol*	*gəzhet*	'grandfather'	*kəka*	'grandmother'
all of G-2	*gəzhet*		*kəka*	

The criterion is only marginally applicable, but it is the particular terms to which it is applicable that call for explanation (see below).

When classified according to the criterion of affinity, Angas terms fall into the groups presented in (5):

(5)	Male Ego		Female Ego	
restricted to consanguineal	*mal*	'sister'	*mal*	
	mol	'brother'	*mol*	
	ɗyem	'son'	*ɗyem*	
	rip	'daughter'	*rip*	
	kən	'uncle'	*kən*	
restricted to affinal	*màt*	'wife'	*màt*	
	sər	'in-law'	*sər*	
			məs	'husband'

(5) cont.

non-restricted	*gəzhet*	'grandfather'	*gəzhet*
	kəka	'grandmother'	*kəka*
	pup	'father'	*pup*
	nən	'mother'	*nən*

Regarding those terms which are not restricted according to the criterion of affinity, the pair *gəzhet* 'grandfather' and *kəka* 'grandmother' are used by the respective sexes to refer to affinal relatives in G-1 and to all consanguineal kinsmen in G-2, and by both sexes to refer to both consanguineal and affinal relatives in G2. Similarly the terms *pup* 'father' and *nən* 'mother' are used to refer to both the siblings of Ego's Mo and Fa (and Mo and Fa themselves) in a consanguineal relationship, and to the mates of those siblings in an affinal relationship. Again, the principle is widely applicable.

It is clear, then, that by discussing Angas kinship and affinal terms from the point of view of Kroeber's principles of relationship a great deal of information can be discovered. In fact, to a very large extent those terms which appear to be exceptional in terms of the principles in that they do not follow the pattern of the majority of terms are readily explainable by recourse to a subsidiary principle which Murdock (1949:104) defines as polarity, or reciprocity.[11] This principle refers to the kin terms which are employed by the kinsmen in a given relationship in referring to each other. The listing in (6) represents the reciprocal terms used by kinsmen in each relationship:

(6)

Relative A		Relative B	
kəka	'grandmother'	*kəka*	
gəzhet	'grandfather'	*gəzhet*	
sər	'in-law'	*sər*	
kən	'uncle'	*kən*	
nən	'mother'	*kyem/rip*	'son/daughter'
pup	'father'	*ɗyem/rip*	'son/daughter'
mal/mol	'sister/brother'	*mal/mol*	
mát	'wife'	*məs*	'husband'

That is, if Relative A refers to Relative B as *kəka*, Relative B will also use the term *kəka* when referring to Relative A. It will be noted that four of the terms are thus bi-directional in their application.[12] For terms which are not bi-directional in the chart, the basis for having two terms is that of sex. I should point out that while the term *mát* 'wife' is restricted to female affines, the reciprocal term *məs* 'husband' is not so restricted but is used to refer to both males and females. This is so because of the nature of the reciprocity principle which is under discussion. The term *məs* is used by Relative B whenever Relative A refers to B as *mát*. Regarding Figures 1 and 2 I mentioned that *mát* is used to refer to one's own wife and the wives of anyone referred to as *mol* 'brother'. Female Ego

[11]Murdock attributes this principle to Kroeber and Lowie.

[12]The terms *mal* and *mol* may seem to be bi-directional as well, in that they appear to be reciprocal when used between siblings of the same sex, but the fact that different terms are used between siblings of different sex points up the fact that they are not genuinely reciprocal.

has no wife of her own, of course, but she still refers to wives of her *mol* kinsmen as *màt* and is thus referred to as *məs* by them. On the contrary, however, male Ego is not referred to as *màt* by anyone (as female Ego is by her husband's brothers), and thus he does not use the term *məs* to refer to anyone either. Thus *màt* is restricted to affines of the female sex, while *məs* is used to refer to both male and female affines.[13]

From the data contained in (6) the difference in usage of kin-terms by male and female Ego can be explained. At level G-2, male Ego uses the term *gəzhet* 'grandfather' to apply to all kinsmen and mates of kinsmen at that generational level. But this follows naturally from the fact that he is in the same relationship to them as his mother's father and father's father and their male siblings are to him. Just as he refers to male consanguineal kinsmen of generation G2 as *gəzhet*, so those of G-2 refer to him as *gəzhet* and have the term applied by him reciprocally to them as well. The term *kəka* 'grandmother' is applied in precisely the same way by female Ego. Thus what appears to be a difference in the use of kinship terminology by male and female Ego turns out to be completely regular.

The same principle of reciprocity applies also to the use of the term *kən* 'uncle'. It is used by both male and female Ego to refer to MoBr, but it has reciprocal application. Male Ego stands in precisely the MoBr relationship to any offspring of someone he refers to as *mal* 'sister'; thus he is referred to by them as *kən*, and he applies the term reciprocally to them as well. The fact that female Ego does not use the term in reference to kinsmen of generation level G-1 can be attributed simply to the fact that, being female, she can never stand in MoBr relationship to anyone; thus she is never called *kən* by anyone in generation G-1, and so she never applies the term to anyone in that generation either.

It should be noted that in both of these cases of reciprocity it is the older kinsman who "defines" the relationship terminologically. It is by virtue of this conceptualization that the apparent differences between male and female kin-term usage can be explained.[14]

3. FORMALIZATION

Lounsbury (1964a) points out that there are two methods of accounting for multiple denotata of a single lexical item. This is true of whatever semantic field in which it occurs, including kinship terminology. The two methods are by means of what he calls "total class definitions" (by which I understand a simple listing of the various semantic application of the terms), or by means of what he calls "basic member definitions", with supplementary "rules of extension". I will follow the latter course here as it gives a rather clear explanation of the working of the Angas kinship system, and it also invites some possibility for language comparison. This section of the paper, then, will consist of proposing basic meanings for the kin-terms and accounting for the extension of their use beyond kinsmen covered by the basic meanings.[15]

---

[13]This is particularly striking because of the apparently inherent male connotation of the term otherwise. Note Angas *goməs* 'male' (< *go* 'person' + *məs*), Sura *mish* 'man', Hausa *na-miji* 'male', Ngizim *gə-msək* 'male', Margi *məshkə̃r* 'younger brother'.

[14]The distribution of the terms *gəzhet* 'grandfather' and *kəka* 'grandmother' in generation level G-1 will be discussed below.

[15]Investigation of any possible cultural motivation for the rules of extension to be proposed remains to be carried out. It is a topic well worthy of consideration.

There are at least three formal systems which have been proposed for analyzing kinterms. Lounsbury (1964a, 1964b) proposes a system using symbols for male and female, as well as abbreviations for major relationships, e.g. F for "father", B for "brother", etc. These symbols are combined (so that MB represents "mother's brother"), and various expansion rules are formulated to account for the extension of the symbol combinations to more distant relationships. The rules proposed contain references both to kinsmen themselves and to linking kinsmen.

Wordick (1975) has as his major focus that of proving that different rules of extension are valid for Sirionó than have been proposed elsewhere. As a result he does not actually propose a formalism; he uses basically a Lounsbury-type model, but he makes a minor change in that he refers to Lounsbury's extension rules as "semantic rules". He mentions also that semantic features could be used in the formulation, and he briefly proposes such contrasts as male vs. female, same generation vs. adjacent generation, family of orientation vs. family of procreation, but he does so only to show the superiority of his own rules to those previously proposed for Sirionó, apparently not as a formalism to be pursued.

Gruber (1973) proposes a formalism which involves lexical decomposition in a manner now familiar through the literature of Generative Semantics. Thus MALE, FEMALE, EXTENDED, OLDER, KIN, OFFSPRING and other concepts are represented as nodes in a derivational tree which are replaced in certain configurations by the lexical items corresponding to the kinterms so designated.

Each of these approaches succeeds in the task of developing the capability of describing kinship systems in a unified way. They all fail in an important way, however, in that the formalisms so developed are not widely applicable to semantic fields other than kinship terminology. That is, each treats the system of kinship terminology as a separate part of language to be described, rather than as an integrated part of the grammar describable in the same way as any other part. Lounsbury's use of the male and female symbols and abbreviations for major kinship relationships is simply not applicable to other semantic fields because such semantic concepts are relevant only to kinship. In the final analysis, Wordick is not really different from Lounsbury in his treatment. It is possible to apply Gruber's proposal to the entire semantic inventory of a language, but only at the cost of the major assumption that every lexical item will be inserted to replace a sub-tree of a derivation. This is a theoretical possibility, of course, but it seems unlikely and involves necessarily a commitment to a theory of syntax that at present is unsubstantiated.[16]

The proposal of this paper is to use semantic features to formalize the Angas system of kinship terminology (in a way similar to that proposed by Wordick, but which he did not carry through on). Such features are of the same nature as well-established syntactic and phonological features, and they are identical in nature to those which have been proposed in the few discussions to date regarding semantics in transformational grammar.[17] In the same way the rules which I will propose as semantic extension rules are identical in form to well established phonological rules. My claim, then, is that the proposals made here are not only equally as adequate as other proposals, but that they have the additional non-trivial advantage of being incorporable into the theory as it is presently formulated, requiring no further apparatus or formalism to be developed. And presumably at least major

[16]To discuss Generative Semantics in detail is well beyond the purpose of this paper. Recent literature is replete with arguments relating to the controversy, to which the reader is referred.

[17]For example, note the use of similar features as "semantic markers" in the earliest work on semantics within transformational grammar (Katz and Fodor, 1963). For a slightly more up-to-date reference see Weinreich (1966) (but note the discussion above regarding my rejection of the hypothesis of lexical decomposition).

parts of the lexicon can be described in similar ways (though apparently with a wide range of feature selection), which would reinforce the assumed integrity of kinship terminology within the entire semantic system.[18]

The Angas language by its use of terms of reference for kinsmen and affines divides up the universe of humanity into four groups. The first division is a group which can be described as "relatives", consisting of one's kinsmen and affinal relatives, who are grouped together by use of the terms discussed in this paper; this group is opposed to the rest of humanity, who are not referred to by kinterms. The second division is between one's consanguineal kinsmen, and all affinal relatives. The third division is between affinal relatives who are mates of oneself or of kinsmen of one's own and of ascending generations, and all other affinal relatives. We may propose the features [+rel] to characterize all "relatives" so defined, [+kin] to characterize kinsmen, and [+in-law] to characterize the second group of affinal relatives described above. The four groups can thus be charted as in (7):

(7)

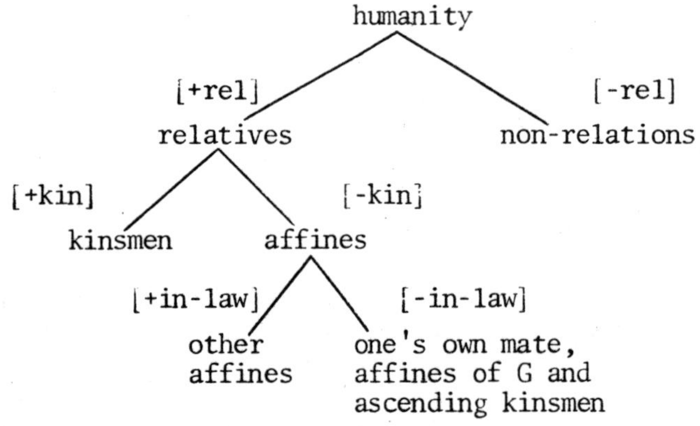

That is, in this proposal all kinsmen and affinal relatives carry the feature [+rel]; all true kinsmen carry in addition the feature [+kin], with all affinal relatives carrying the feature [-kin]; and one's own mate, and affines of kinsmen of one's own and ascending generations carry the feature [-in-law]. The motivation behind these feature specifications will be seen in the discussion below; it is of significance here simply to notice that affines of descending generations are treated differently from the point of view of the lexicon from those of other generations, and that consanguineal and affinal relatives are treated differently also. The feature [rel] will not concern us further here in that the subject matter of the paper is limited strictly to kinsmen and affinal relatives (all of whom carry the feature [+rel]).

The lists in (8) show the different relatives who are referred to by each particular term in Angas, within the limits of the data covered by the charts in Figures 1 and 2:[19]

(8) *kəka* FaMo, FaMoSi, FaMoBrWi, FaFaBrWi, FaFaSi, MoMo, MoMoSi, MoMoBrWi, MoFaBrWi, MoFaSi, MoMoMo, MoFaMo, FaFaMo, FaMoMo, SoWi (female Ego only)

[18]This may prove to be a gratuitous assumption, but I think not. Rather I expect further research to reveal that large portions of the lexicon are arranged in semantic fields which are describable in terms similar to those proposed here.

[19]In the listing for *gəzhet* and *kəka*, the designation SoWi is used as a cover term for all wives of kinsmen referred to as *mol* 'brother'. The restriction of the last portion of the list for *ɗyem* and *rip* to female Ego is a result of the inapplicability of the term *kən* 'uncle' for descending generations when a female reference point is used.

(8) cont.

gəzhet	FaFa, FaFaBr, FaFaSiHu, FaMoSiHu, FaMoBr, MoFa, MoFaBr, MoFaSiHu, MoMoSiHu, MoMoBr, MoMoFa, MoFaFa, FaFaFa, FaMoFa, SoWi (male Ego only)
nən	Mo, MoSi, MoBrWi, FaSi, FaBrWi
pup	Fa, FaBr, FaSiHu, MoSiHu
kən	MoBr
mal	Si, FaBrDa, FaSiDa, MoSiDa, MoBrDa
mol	Br, FaBrSo, FaSiSo, MoSiSo, MoBrSo
mât	Wi, BrWi, FaBrSoWi, FaSiSoWi, MoSiSoWi, MoBrSoWi
məs	Hu, HuSi, HuBr[20]
sər	all affines but Hu, HuBr, HuSi of G, and all male affines of G-1
d̃yem	So, BrSo, FaBrSoSo, FaSiSoSo, MoSiSoSo, MoBrSoSo; SiSo, FaBrDaSo, FaSiDaSo, MoSiDaSo, MoBrDaSo (after semicolon female Ego only)
rip	Da, BrDa, FaBrSoDa, FaSiSoDa, MoSiSoDa, MoBrSoDa; SiDa, FaBrDaDa, FaSiDaDa, MoSiDaDa, MoBrDaDa (after semicolon female Ego only)

Now, how shall the "basic member definitions" be chosen from the possibilities apparent in the list, and how shall they be represented? I shall choose here to represent all relatives in terms of what I shall call "semantic distinctive features". Further, I shall choose as the basic meaning that relative referred to by each term who is closest to Ego, "closest" being defined as nearest to the nuclear family, i.e. the fewest "branches" of the tree from Ego. This may be somewhat ethnocentric, since it is conceivable that there may be an argument for taking another parameter as being more basic in some universal sense. But the position I take here is in accord with others who have worked in this field, including Radcliffe-Brown and Forde. In establishing relative orders (degrees) of relationship among kinsmen, they say (1950:6):

> "Relationships of the first order are those within the elementary family, viz. the relation of parent and child, that of husband and wife, and that between siblings. Relationships of the second order are those traced through one connecting person such as those with father's father, mother's brother, . . . etc. Those of the third order have two connecting links, as mother's brother's son, father's sister's husband, and so on. So we can go on to the fourth, fifty, or *n*th order."

That they are speaking here of proximity of relationship is brought out further when they say (p. 9):

> ". . . there are necessarily distinctions between near and distant relatives included in the same category. Thus amongst the men referred to as 'father' the nearest relative is, of course, the actual 'own' father. After him come

[20]The inclusion of HuBr in the listing for *məs* is based upon extrapolation from the data in Figures 1 and 2 in accordance with earlier discussion regarding reciprocity.

> his brothers and after them his parallel first cousins and perhaps in some systems the husbands of the mother's sisters. So on to more and more distant relatives of the same terminological category."

We may note further that Lounsbury (1964b) states that to take the nuclear family members as being the most elementary follows both Murdock and Malinowski, and that it is proper to conceive of extensions of the terms to more distant relatives. I conclude then that the glosses which have been proposed are satisfactory as basic meanings.

In developing the scheme of features, let us first restrict our discussion to kinsmen, setting aside affines temporarily. We saw above (1)-(5) that the semantic parameters of generation, collaterality, sex of kinsman, and affinity are employed in the system of Angas kinship terminology, with sex of linking kinsman used in one instance (to distinguish MoBr from FaBr). We have seen further that because of the reciprocal application of some terms the sex of Ego has no effect on kin-terms employed (I have not yet dealt with SoWi and equivalent terms), so that the distinction in the charts between male and female Ego need no longer be maintained. Translating the parameter of collaterality into its obverse of lineality, we may represent the features of sex, affinity, and lineality for Angas kin-terms as in (9):[21]

(9)	male	lineal	affinal
gəzhet	+	+	-
kəka	-	+	-
pup	+	+	-
nən	-	+	-
kən	+	-	-
mol	+	+	-
mal	-	+	-
dyem	+	+	-
rip	-	+	-

That is, being kinsmen, none of these are affinal in their basic meaning, consistent distinctions are made in terms of sex, and all except for MoBr are lineal rather than collateral.[22] The parameter of generation will require three features to distinguish the five generations which it is necessary to speak about. Although this is inefficient use of binary features (three features can make up to eight such distinctions), under this approach there is no alternative. We may thus propose the three features [G] to denote kinsmen of Ego's generation and thus distinguish them from all others, [ascending] to distinguish ascending from descending generations, and [distant] to distinguish those generations more than one generation removed from Ego from those only one removed. Adding these features to the matrix of (9) will result in (10):

[21]These lexical specifications include also [+rel, +kin] in accordance with the above discussion of course; I have omitted such features here for simplicity.

[22]I am aware that the lineal-collateral dichotomy is only of marginal application within the Angas system, but it will be useful in the extension rules I will propose. Further, I am attempting to provide a set of universally applicable constructs, and the distinction will obviously be necessary for systems of all but the Hawaiian type.

(10)

	male	lineal	affinal	G	ascending	distant
gəzhet	+	+	-	-	+	+
kəka	-	+	-	-	+	+
pup	+	+	-	-	+	-
nən	-	+	-	-	+	-
kən	+	-	-	-	+	-
mol	+	+	-	+	-	-
mal	-	+	-	+	-	-
ɗyem	+	+	-	-	-	-
rip	-	+	-	-	-	-

These then represent the basic lexical features of the kin-terms which are relevant to their application to the universe of kinsmen and affines. It is a fact that in Angas no specific lexical term is marked [-G, -ascending, +distant]; this would be the specification of kinsmen in the G-2 generation level, and the absence of such terms in Angas is a result of the reciprocal application of the G2 terms at that level. Note that in the basic member definitions it is not necessary to choose arbitrarily between MoFa and FaFa as the basic rendering for *gəzhet*. Both of these relations are covered by the features as given; that is, a lineal male relative of G2 generation.

Obviously, a good bit of redundancy among the features exists in the Angas system; there are only nine terms involved, and the six features required semantically could theoretically make over five hundred distinctions if maximally efficient in their application. There is first a group of logical redundancies which would be in effect in whatever system the same features were used with the same definitions. These may be listed as follows:

(11) [+ascending]
↓
[-G]
|
(12) [+G]
↓
[-ascending]

(13) [+in-law]
↓
[+rel, -kin]

(14) [+kin]
↓
[+rel]

That is, no term can belong to more than one generation level, so (11) and (12) exclude the specifications [G] and [ascending] from each other. Secondly, in line with the chart in (7), certain obligatory relations hold among the features [rel], [kin], and [in-law]. The redundancy rules (11)-(14) will hold for any kinship system using the same features in the same way.

In addition there are two redundancy rules which are specific in the application to the Angas system as described above. These are as follows:

(15) [+distant]
↓
[+ascending]

(16) [-ascending]
↓
[-distant]

That is, because of the fact that G-2 terms are reciprocals, no G-2 level lexical terms exist as such; therefore, if a term is [+distant] it is necessarily [+ascending] as well, and if it is [-ascending] it is necessarily [-distant] as well. These rules are specific to Angas and would not apply to all systems.

Incorporating these redundancies into the matrix of (10) results in the revised matrix for the lexical items as shown in (17):

(17)

	male	lineal	affinal	G	ascending	distant
gəzhet	+	+	-			+
kəka	-	+	-			+
pup	+	+	-		+	-
nən	-	+	-		+	-
kən	+	-	-		+	-
mol	+	+	-	+		
mal	-	+	-	+		
ɗyem	+	+	-	-	-	
rip	-	+	-	-	-	

The redundancy rules (11)-(16) will then fill in the matrices properly to produce (10).[23]

Now, how can the extension rules be formulated? It would seem that Kroeber's parameters, or something like them, can be used to characterize ALL kinsmen, no matter how distant.[24] Of course, not each individual can be distinguished from all others since the number of kinsmen of each Ego, while not infinite, is larger than eight features can handle (note

[23]It would seem to be the case that a further redundancy rule exists between the features [lineal] and [affinal] so that any term which is [-lineal] is also marked as [-affinal]. But it will be necessary below to make a distinction among affinal relatives which parallels the lineal-collateral distinction for kinsmen, so it is not possible to affirm a rule of that nature. Whether such a distinction is valid or useful beyond the Angas kinship system is presently unclear; it may be the case that such a rule would be possible in another system.

[24]In fact, this seems to be precisely what Kroeber intended. He says in introducing his principles (1909:239): "It is apparent that what we should try to deal with is not the hundreds or thousands of slightly varying relationships that are expressed or can be expressed by the various languages of man, but the principles or categories of relationship which underlie these."

Kroeber's "hundreds or thousands"). But it would seem to be true that it is simply not necessary to distinguish each individual from each other. That is, we may conceive of the universe of relatives as similar to phonetic data: just as each occurrence of [a] is not distinguished as to duration, exact placement, voice quality, etc. (although it is often claimed that no two utterances are exactly identical), neither is each individual relative distinguished.[25] Rather, in both cases we may consider some of the differentiating minutiae as being irrelevant ("below the threshold of perception" in acoustic terms), and thus ignorable.

Let us propose, then, that the features given above for Angas kinterms can be used to describe any kinsman, even though the inventory of features is abbreviated in number even from Kroeber, and thus obviously not each kinsman can be separately defined. Our problem then is to demonstrate how the kin-terms which are given in their basic meaning specifications in (10) and (17) can be extended to cover kinsmen having different feature matrices. This will require the alteration of the specification of the kin-term optionally to apply to kinsmen having the differing specifications as required.[26]

The first principle to be captured in the Angas system is that at generation level G2 all collaterals, and all mates of lineal and collateral kinsmen are treated as lineal kinsmen. Or to put it in another way, the terms used to refer to lineal kinsmen are applied also to collaterals, and all mates of lineals and collaterals. The feature matrices of a representative sample of such kinsmen is given in (18):

(18)		male	lineal	affinal	G	ascending	distant
	MoFaBr	+	-	-	-	+	+
	FaMoSiHu	+	-	+	-	+	+
	FaFaBrWi	-	-	+	-	+	+
	FaFaSi	-	-	-	-	+	+

That is, all are defined by the features as being in G2, all are necessarily [-lineal] or they would be the lexical kinsmen themselves, and affines are distinguished from kinsmen, and males from females. Note that the particular affines here would be distinguished from the vast number of others because they are affines of kinsmen of ascending generations, and thus they carry the feature specification [-in-law].

The change that is needed in the basic kin-terms *gəzhet* and *kəka* to extend them to cover these relatives is that they be optionally given the specification [-lineal], with [affinal] being either plus or minus. The rule needed may be formulated as in (19):[27]

---

[25]That is, not by kinterm application. There is great differentiation evident of course in the use of personal names.

[26]Note that what is being proposed here is a set of a type of semantic interpretation rules which operate upon lexical items in the form of basic member definitions, and extend the range of semantic reference of the items to the possible appropriate kinsmen in the real world. As presently defined, *pup* is in the lexicon as referring to father, and father is the only referent which can be assigned to the term by the semantic interpretation rules. But by altering the feature make-up of *pup* by semantic extension rules, we make it possible for its range of referents to be altered to apply to kinsmen other than that encoded in its basic member definition.

[27]The theoretical implications of rules of this type will be discussed in another paper. Basically, I am assuming that each well-defined semantic field has certain features which characterize the lexical items belonging in that field, and that such features are changed by semantic extension rules to extend the basic terms to the universe of that field appropriately.

(19) Grandparent Extension (optional)

$$[+\text{kin}] \rightarrow \begin{bmatrix}-\text{lineal}\\ \alpha\text{affinal}\end{bmatrix} \quad / \quad \begin{bmatrix}\_\_\_\_\\ +\text{distant}\end{bmatrix}$$

That is, given the occurrence of *gəzhet* or *kəka* in a string, I am proposing that semantic interpretation rules may optionally apply rule (19) and thus interpret the referent as being any relative having the feature matrix which results. If the rule is applied, the reference is to non-lineal kinsmen and affines of generation G2; if it is not applied, the reference is to lineal kinsmen of G2 only. Obviously, if the rule is applied the term is multiply ambiguous as to exact referent, but the ambiguity reflects the facts of the case precisely. Thus when someone says 'My *gəzhet* went to Lagos today', we may in fact know exactly which of his male G2 relatives he is referring to, but that is a result of familiarity with the speaker and his situation, not a result of our interpretation of the linguistic facts alone. Note that we are not simply manipulating features here, but by the definition of the features and the formulation of the possible extension we affirm the fact that in the Angas kinship system G2 kinsmen and their mates are all treated as lineal kinsmen, with the terms for lineal kinsmen extended to cover them in reference.

The second principle to be captured is that in G1, except for MoBr, the situation is exactly the same as in G2. The matrix in (20) gives the feature specification of a representative sample of G1 relatives:

(20)	male	lineal	affinal	G	ascending	distant
FaBr	+	-	-	-	+	-
FaSiHu	+	-	+	-	+	-
MoBr	+	-	-	-	+	-
MoBrWi	-	-	+	-	+	-
MoSi	-	-	-	-	+	-

Obviously we have a major problem; FaBr and MoBr are specified identically, but we know that MoBr is *kən* and FaBr is *pup*. What distinguishes them is the sex of the connecting link, as I discussed above. This is very much of a complicating factor in the system, but as we have seen this particular portion of the system is in fact very complicated and matches none of the six most common types of kinship systems (all of which treat MoBr and FaBr in a parallel fashion). It is necessary, then, to add an additional feature to the specification of G1 relatives (at least males) to block the application of the extension rule to keep it from being applied to MoBr; then *pup* can be extended to all other relatives as required, and *kən* will have MoBr as its sole referent (with its reciprocal application, of course). The revised specification of G1 relatives of (20) is given in (21):

(21)	male	lineal	affinal	G	ascending	distant	male link
FaBr	+	-	-	-	+	-	+
FaSiHu	+	-	+	-	+	-	+
MoBr	+	-	-	-	+	-	-
MoBrWi	-	-	+	-	+	-	-
MoSi	-	-	-	-	+	-	-

The lexical specification for *kən* 'uncle' must be expanded to include the specification [-male link]; then the rule required to extend the reference of *pup* can be formulated as follows:

(22) Father Extension (optional)

$$\begin{bmatrix}\text{+kin}\\ \text{+male}\\ \text{+lineal}\end{bmatrix} \longrightarrow \left\{\begin{matrix}\begin{bmatrix}\text{-lineal}\\ \text{+affinal}\\ \text{-kin}\end{bmatrix}\\ \begin{bmatrix}\text{-lineal}\\ \text{+male link}\end{bmatrix}\end{matrix}\right\} \quad / \quad \begin{bmatrix}\rule{2em}{0.4pt}\\ \text{+ascending}\\ \text{-distant}\end{bmatrix}$$

That is, the term *pup*, which is lexically marked as being [+lineal, +male] and is the only one so marked in this generation, may refer not simply to Ego's own father, but also to non-lineal male relatives who have a male link with Ego, i.e. FaBr, and to male mates of collateral kinsmen. The term *kən* will then have the specification [+male, -lineal, -male link] and will not be extended beyond MoBr (which is the only kinsman so specified in the range of the information given in the charts in Figures 1 and 2).

Rule (22) is very complex, but it reflects the complexity of the situation. That is, were it not for the "peculiar" nature of MoBr, i.e. if Angas were a Hawaiian system, the rule could be written identical to that for G2, with the feature [+ascending] replacing [+distant], thus combining the two rules. Or were all aunts and uncles treated as such (as in an Eskimo system), the lexical items referring to them could occur in the lexicon as [-lineal, -in-law], and the reference would be to all uncles without any extension rule. Or if only cross-uncles and -aunts were treated separately but in parallel fashion (as in a Crow-Omaha-Iriquois system), the rule could be written in terms of a feature [parallel] instead of [male link], with the rule much simplified. But the nature of Angas MoBr is very complicating, requiring even a second rule for G1 to handle extension of *nən* 'mother'. This second rule extends the possible reference of the lineal *nən* to cover collaterals and female mates of collaterals at this level, precisely paralleling the rule for G2. We may formulate it as in (23):

(23) Mother Extension (optional)

$$\begin{bmatrix}\text{+kin}\\ \text{-male}\end{bmatrix} \longrightarrow \begin{bmatrix}\text{-lineal}\\ \alpha\text{affinal}\end{bmatrix} \quad / \quad \begin{bmatrix}\rule{2em}{0.4pt}\\ \text{+ascending}\\ \text{-distant}\end{bmatrix}$$

That is, female kin-terms of G1 (*nən* is the only one) may refer to non-lineals and mates of non-lineals.

The third governing principle in the use of Angas kinship terminology is that consanguineal kinsmen of Ego's generation are all treated as lineals; that is, lineal terms may be extended to refer to collateral kinsmen as well. The rule to perform this extension is given in (24):

(24) Sibling Extension (optional)

$$[\text{+kin}] \longrightarrow [\text{-lineal}] \quad / \quad \begin{bmatrix}\rule{2em}{0.4pt}\\ \text{+G}\end{bmatrix}$$

That is, kin-terms of generation level G may optionally be extended to refer to non-lineal kinsmen (but not affines). Some representative kinsmen of G are given in feature-specification matrix form in (25):

(25)	male	lineal	affinal	G	ascending	distant
MoSiSo	+	-	-	+	-	-
FaBrSo	+	-	-	+	-	-
FaSiDa	-	-	-	+	-	-
MoBrDa	-	-	-	+	-	-

Rule (24) can be optionally applied to extend the reference of *mol* 'brother' and *mal* 'sister' to cover these kinsmen.

The fourth extension rule required regarding kinsmen is that the terms *dyem* 'son' and *rip* 'daughter' may be extended to refer to the children of one's siblings (remember the restriction regarding MoBr in its reciprocal application for male Ego in G-1). A representative sample of such kinsmen is given in (26):

(26)	male	lineal	affinal	G	ascending	distant
BrSo	+	-	-	-	-	-
BrDa	-	-	-	-	-	-
FaBrSoDa	-	-	-	-	-	-
FaBrDaDa	-	-	-	-	-	-
MoSiDaSo	+	-	-	-	-	-
MoBrSoSo	+	-	-	-	-	-

The rule required is, of course, identical with that used at generation level G, with the exception that features for generation are specified differently:

(27) Child Extension (optional)

$$[+\text{kin}] \longrightarrow [-\text{lineal}] \quad / \quad \begin{bmatrix} \underline{\qquad} \\ -\text{G} \\ -\text{ascending} \\ -\text{distant} \end{bmatrix}$$

This rule has the same function as that of (24) for this generation.

It should be emphasized that all five of these semantic rules, i.e. (19), (22), (23), (24), and (27), are of the same nature, serving in one way or another to rewrite the feature [+lineal] as specified in the lexicon as [-lineal], thus extending the semantic reference. This reflects the fact that in Angas the major principle in effect is that of equating collaterals and mates of collaterals with lineals, applicable at all generations. The major complications arise at the level of G1 because of MoBr, with the additional restriction that mates are not included in the equation for generations G and G-1. It seems to be the case that once a person, e.g. FaBr, is identified as *pup* 'father', his children logically are referred to as siblings and his wife as *nən* 'mother'. If this characterization could be formalized, a considerable savings in complexity would result. This is in fact what Lounsbury has attempted to do, but his use of a mechanism and formalism applicable to only kinship terminology makes his treatment restricted from applying to the semantics of language generally. I have attempted in this presentation to formulate a model which will be widely applicable, but I am unable in the process to capture (except by rule comparison and possible combination) the overall generality.

The remaining extensions to be noted extend the reference of affinal terms. The first principle is that the wife of anyone referred to as *mol* 'brother' is referred to as *màt* 'wife'. The terms *màt* and *məs* have the feature matrices shown in (28):

(28)	in-law	male	lineal	affinal	G	ascending	distant
màt	-	-	+	+	+	-	-
məs	-	+	+	+	+	-	-

I am using the feature combination [+lineal, +affinal] here to denote the fact that the relative so designated is *himself* the mate of Ego or of Ego's kinsman, not merely a link to a more distant affine. The more distant affines, e.g. BrWiMo, etc., on the other hand, are marked as [-lineal, +affinal], denoting their more distant, non-lineal (in terms of Ego's kinsmen) relationship. This is not the normal anthropological use of "lineal", but such a distinction is a useful one and the concept of lineality does in fact seem to be relevant. The extended relatives who are terminologically grouped with *màt* include the following, shown with their matrices:

(29)	in-law	male	lineal	affinal	G	ascending	distant
BrWi	-	-	+	+	+	-	-
FaBrSoWi	-	-	+	+	+	-	-
FaSiSoWi	-	-	+	+	+	-	-
MoSiSoWi	-	-	+	+	+	-	-
MoBrSoWi	-	-	+	+	+	-	-

All of these relatives are [-in-law] by virtue of the fact that they are mates of kinsmen of generation G. Thus they match the appropriate features of *màt* and the term will cover them semantically in its primary reference with no extension necessary.

The second principle regarding affines is that the term *məs* 'husband' is extended to refer to some more distant affines in addition to its primary reference to Hu himself (including some female relatives). A representative sample of such relatives is given in (30):

(30)	in-law	male	lineal	affinal	G	ascending	distant
Hu	-	+	+	+	+	-	-
HuSi	+	-	-	+	+	-	-
HuBr	+	+	-	+	+	-	-
HuFaBrDa	+	-	-	+	+	-	-
HuMoSiDa	+	-	-	+	+	-	-

Not being mates of either Ego or kinsmen of Ego in ascending generation, these relatives are all [+in-law], and some are male, some female. Note that again the feature combination [+lineal, +affinal] is used to distinguish, for example, SiHu (which is *sər*) from HuSi (which is *məs*), which carries the features [-lineal, +affinal]. The rule needed here must extend the term *məs* 'husband', lexically specified as [-kin, -in-law, +male, +lineal], to cover the relatives listed in (30). And the term to be so extended must be restricted to apply only to *məs*. The necessary rule may be formulated as follows:

(31) Husband Extension (optional)

$$\begin{bmatrix}-\text{kin}\\+\text{male}\\+\text{lineal}\end{bmatrix} \longrightarrow \begin{bmatrix}\alpha\text{male}\\-\text{lineal}\\+\text{in-law}\end{bmatrix} \quad / \quad \begin{bmatrix}\overline{}\\+\text{G}\end{bmatrix}$$

That is, the term *məs*, being a non-kinship term but marked as denoting a lineal relationship as described above (as the mate of Ego), may be extended to refer to an in-law who is more distant (not a mate of Ego or of Ego's kinsmen) of generation G.

To this point I have not discussed the application of kin-terms to SoWi and comparable relatives, and it is to this problem that I turn now. These relatives are treated terminologically as identical to all kinsmen of level G-2. What makes the problem difficult is that G-2 itself is a reciprocal relationship defined by Ego, so that Ego stands in precisely the same relationship to G-2 and G2 relatives. Earlier in this paper I have defined the terms *kəka* 'grandmother' and *gəzhet* 'grandfather' as being lexically G2 terms; now they must be extended to apply to specific affinal relatives at the G-1 level.

It seems that the neatest treatment conceptually would be to treat these G-1 relatives as being identified as equivalent to G-2 relatives. This will give the correct result in every instance, and it has the additional advantage of graphically providing possible motivation for the identity of such terms, at least in a limited way. I have no evidence that this is in fact the motivation, but by equating terminologically SoWi and comparable relatives with lineal kinsmen an incest taboo is invoked (for male Ego) which would make any instance of illicit sexual relations with such relatives an unmistakable act of incest; terminologically, SoWi is actually *gəzhet* 'grandfather/granddaughter', and sexual relations between such kinsmen are prohibited culturally. Under such a hypothesis the pattern for female Ego would have arisen analogically. Terminological identity, then, may be the means by which a potentially sexually charged situation can be defused. If this is in fact the case, an analysis which shows this formally is to be preferred.

But a major problem arises (in addition to the lack of any genuine evidence for such an analysis). My purpose in this paper has been to provide a pattern of lexical specifications and extension which begins with the feature make-up of the lexical item and by semantic rules extends its reference by alteration of the feature make-up. But the analysis discussed above requires just the opposite approach, viz. that of beginning with the "etic" referents and redefining them to match the lexical specification. The approach developed so far is more in keeping with the present formal mechanisms within linguistic theory, e.g. phonological rules change underlying specifications to produce phonetic manifestation, not the other way around, and it is in fact totally adquate, even if the above conjuctural statements are to be taken advantage of.

The important fact is that *gəzhet* and *kəka* are reciprocal terms, and that their usage is defined by the sex of the relative of the older generation. The conceptualization needed, then, is the equation of HuFa and FaFa/MoFa, and of HuMo and FaMo/MoMo. In terms of semantic extension rules, such a conceptualization can be achieved in exactly the opposite way, with the kin-terms *gəzhet* and *kəka* extended to apply to HuFa and HuMo respectively.

The relatives which are to be covered by these G2 terms include the following:

(32)	male	lineal	affinal	G	ascending	distant
HuMo	-	-	+	-	+	-
HuFa	+	-	+	-	+	-
HuFaFaBrSo	+	-	+	-	+	-

(32) cont.	male	lineal	affinal	G	ascending	distant
HuMoMoSiSo	+	-	+	-	+	-
HuFaFaBrDa	-	-	+	-	+	-

By contrast, *gəzhet* and *kəka* carry lexical features as follows:

(33)	male	lineal	affinal	G	ascending	distant
gəzhet	+	+	-	-	+	+
kəka	-	+	-	-	+	+

The rule which is needed must change the feature specification for [lineal] and [affinal] (so that the reference is extended from lineal kinsmen to affinal relatives), and the specification for [distant] (so that reference is extended from G2 to G1). The rule may be formulated as follows:

(34) Daughter-in-Law Rule (optional)

$$\begin{bmatrix} \alpha\text{male} \\ +\text{lineal} \\ -\text{affinal} \\ +\text{distant} \end{bmatrix} \longrightarrow \begin{bmatrix} -\text{lineal} \\ +\text{affinal} \\ -\text{distant} \end{bmatrix}$$

This rule is formally unsatisfying because it requires the specification of some of the same features on both sides of the arrow. This is a result of the fact that the specification of the term to be extended semantically must be made very precise, and it happens to be the case that the same features which are necessary to achieve the required precision are the same ones which change in the extension. The proposed rule will change the feature specification appropriately, with the principle of reciprocal application (the nature of the relationship being defined by the older of the relatives involved) extending it to the reciprocal kinsmen as required.

The final problem which remains is that of providing for the semantic interpretation of *sər* 'in-law'. I noted earlier that the term refers widely to affinal relatives who are not themselves the mates of Ego's kinsmen (see (7)). We may propose then that *sər* carries the lexical feature [+in-law] which is common to all such affinal relatives.[28] But Figures 1 and 2 show that it is used also to refer to husbands of women referred to as *mal* 'sister'. A representative sample of such relatives is presented in (35):

(35)	in-law	male	lineal	affinal	G	ascending	distant
SiHu	-	+	+	+	+	-	-
MoSiDaHu	-	+	+	+	+	-	-
FaSiDaHu	-	+	+	+	+	-	-
MoBrDaHu	-	+	+	+	+	-	-
FaBrDaHu	-	+	+	+	+	-	-

---

[28]It may be that a more basic definition can be proposed, one which takes one such relative as the basic definition as in the other terms, but I know of no motivation for such a proposal; if so, it would make the overall system more consistent.

A second group referred to as *sər* 'in-law' are husbands of women referred to as *rip* 'daughter' and *kən* 'uncle' (in the case of male Ego only). A representative sample of such relatives is shown in (36):

(36)	in-law	male	lineal	affinal	G	ascending	distant
DaHu	-	+	+	+	-	-	-
BrDaHu	-	+	+	+	-	-	-
FaBrSoDaHu	-	+	+	+	-	-	-
MoSiDaDaHu	-	+	+	+	-	-	-

It is striking that the matrices of (35) and (36) match precisely, with the sole exception of the feature [G]. We may formulate an extension rule to apply to the lexical matrix of *sər* 'in-law' to extend it to such relatives optionally as follows:

(37) In-law Extension (optional)

$$[\text{+in-law}] \longrightarrow \begin{bmatrix} \text{-in-law} \\ \text{+male} \\ \text{+lineal} \\ \text{+affinal} \\ \alpha\text{G} \\ \text{-ascending} \\ \text{-distant} \end{bmatrix}$$

4. SUMMARY

I have in this paper outlined a means by which the terminological classification of kinsmen in the Angas system of kinship terminology can be accounted for, using widely accepted anthropological criteria as parameters translated into features. I am making the claim that other kinship systems can be accounted for by means of the identical formalism, although of course the details will differ. Other formalizaitons have been proposed, but the one I present here has the non-trivial advantage of requiring no new formalism within the theoretical model.

The major principle of Angas kinship terminology is that collateral kinsmen and their mates (with some generational restrictions) are treated as lineal kinsmen. This is seen clearly in the semantic extension rules I have formulated in the formal specification of kin-terms (lexically [+lineal]) as [-lineal] after application of the rule involved (see especially (19), (22), (23), (24), (27)). These rules could probably be combined into a single super-rule to show this fact more clearly formally, but I have preferred to keep them distinct in this presentation for clarity. Also I could have made a blanket statement to the effect that all these semantic extension rules are optional, but I have preferred to mark each one as optional as it is presented in this discussion to make its optionality consistently obvious to the reader. The kin-terms in fact have a referent in their lexical form; the rules simply show that the reference MAY be extended to other relatives.

5. FUTURE RESEARCH

Some beginning work has been done in comparative Chadic studies from the point of view of phonology (especially Newman and Ma (1966)) and syntax (especially Schuh (1971) and Newman and Schuh (1974)), but to my knowledge little has been done in semantics.

Kinship terminologies offer a good opportunity for semantic investigations. First, the universe of kinsmen is the same in every culture, so that the same etic units can be compared cross-culturally with no distortion of the facts. Second, by necessity each language is forced to classify this universe of kinsmen into a comparatively small number of terminological groupings, thus imposing some degree of organization upon them. To the extent that language and culture form congruent systems, this organization will reflect the social organization, at least at the time of formulation. Third, it would seem from the literature that the major parameters relevant in kinship classification are fairly well established, so that the semantic features required to represent this organization may be at hand; in that the universe of kinsmen is the same in all cultures, it would follow that the features would necessarily be virtually the same for all languages (I have mentioned some possible differences in the discussion). Thus an ideal area of comparison is assured.

Such a comparative project would need to proceed along two fronts to be maximally useful—first, establishing cognate terms and reconstructing proto-Chadic forms;[29] second, reconstructing proto-Chadic basic member definitions and semantic extension rules for the terms. This is so because all of the following situations might be expected to be found: Language A and Language B may or may not have cognate terms; if the terms are cognate they may or may not have the same referent as basic member definition, and even if they are not cognate the two non-cognate terms may have the same basic referent (or of course they may not); and if the terms (whether cognate or non-cognate) have the same referent, they may or may not have the same rules of extension.

For example, Angas *pup* 'father' appears on inspection to be cognate with Hausa *uba* 'father'.[30] Further, they both seem to have the same basic referent (actual father of Ego). But are the rules of extension the same? Does Hausa *uba* have precisely the same range of meaning as Angas *pup*? Specifically, is there a Hausa word comparable to Angas *kən* 'uncle' which is used instead of *uba* to refer to MoBr? If the extension rules are not the same, which can be proposed as being closer to the proto-Chadic rule, and which derived? Can the formal content of the rules of extension give any help in determing which rule is prior? Can the feature changes themselves tell us anything of a theoretical nature regarding the nature of semantic change?

Or note Angas *mol* 'brother'. Obviously it is not cognate with Hausa *ɗanuwa* 'brother'. But more than that, Angas *mol* is apparently mono-morphemic, while Hausa *ɗanuwa* is composed of *ɗa* 'son' and *uwa* 'mother', so that its meaning literally is 'mother's son'. Here we have an additional question, whether proto-Chadic kin-terms are more characteristically mono-morphemic or compounds. Compounding would seem to be the pattern in this particular case because Sura (which is very closely related to Angas) also has what appears to be a compound form for 'brother' (apparently similar to Hausa in construction). Note in addition that Margi *mwal* means 'friend'; is this form cognate with Angas *mol*? If so, which carries the meaning of the proto-Chadic form (if in fact either one does), and which is derived?[31]

[29]This has a beginning in Newman and Ma (1966); they reconstruct **s-r-* as meaning 'in-law', a form obviously the source for the Angas *sər* with the same meaning.

[30]I present this only as an example, not as a statement of cognate status. It may rather be another example of similar phonological sequences being used to refer to one's parents in near-universal patterns in languages of the world.

[31]Although less likely, Margi *mwal* 'friend' may instead be cognate with Angas *mal* 'sister'.

Can data from languages of other branches of Afroasiatic shed light on such questions?

It may be the case in the particular application to Chadic languages that from a purely linguistic point of view we can learn nothing from such investigations. This would be the case if the hypothesis that present-day Chadic languages have resulted from the adoption of eastern languages by African cultures should be true. In such a situation the linguistic data is likely to be simply an overlay superimposed on the social structure, and we would expect no match lexically because one would not necessarily be expected culturally either. Nevertheless the subject is worthy of investigation. I have tried to suggest that it may hold potential for theoretical insights also.

REFERENCES

Burquest, D.A. 1971. *A Preliminary Study of Angas Phonology*. Studies in Nigerian Languages 1. Zaria, Nigeria: Institute of Linguistics.

______________. 1973. "A Grammar of Angas." Doctoral dissertation, UCLA.

Gruber, Jeffrey S. 1973. " H̀õã kinship terms." *Linguistic Inquiry* 4:427-49.

Hoffmann, Carl. 1963. *A Grammar of the Margi Language*. London: Oxford University Press.

Jungraithmayr, Herrmann. 1963. "On the ambiguous position of Angas." *Journal of African Languages* 2:272-78.

______________. 1964a. "Die Sprache der Sura (Maghavul) im Nordnigerien." *Afrika und Übersee* 47:8-89, 204-20.

______________. 1964b. "Texte und Sprichwörter im Angas von Kabwir (Nordnigerien)." *Afrika und Übersee* 48:114-27.

Katz, Jerrold J., and Jerry A. Fodor. 1963. "The structure of a semantic theory." *Language* 39:170-210.

Kroeber, Alfred L. 1909. "Classificatory systems of relationship." *Journal of the Royal Anthropological Institute* 39:77-84. [Reprinted in Morton H. Fried (ed.), *Readings in Anthropology*, vol. ii. N.Y.: Thomas Y. Crowell Co., 1959.]

Lounsbury, Floyd G. 1964a. "The structural analysis of kinship semantics." *Proceedings of the Ninth International Congress of Linguists*, pp. 1073-1090. [Reprinted in Stephen A. Tyler (ed.), *Cognitive Anthropology*. N.Y.: Holt, Rinehart and Winston, 1969.]

______________. 1964b. "A formal account of the Crow- and Omaha-type kinship terminologies." In W.H. Goodenough (ed.), *Explorations in Cultural Anthropology*. N.Y.: McGraw-Hill, 1964. [Reprinted in Stephen A. Tyler (ed.), *Cognitive Anthropology*. N.Y.: Holt, Rinehart and Winston, 1969.]

Mohr, Richard. 1958. "Zur sozialen Organisation der Angas in Nord-Nigeria." *Anthropos* 53:547-71.

Murdock, George Peter. 1949. *Social Structure*. N.Y.: The Macmillan Co.

Newman, Paul. 1970. *A Grammar of Tera*. Berkeley: University of California Press.

Newman, Paul, and Roxana Ma. 1966. "Comparative Chadic: phonology and lexicon." *Journal of African Languages* 5:218-51.

Newman, Paul, and Russell G. Schuh. 1974. "The Hausa aspect system" *Afroasiatic Linguistics* 1:1-39.

Radcliffe-Brown, A.R., and Daryll Forde, editors. 1950. *African Systems of Kinship and Marriage*. London: Oxford University Press.

Schuh, Russell G. 1971. "Reconstruction of the syntax of subject emphasis in certain Chadic languages." *Studies in African Linguistics*, supplement 2, pp. 67-77.

Schusky, Ernest L. 1965. *Manual for Kinship Analysis*. N.Y.: Holt, Rinehart and Winston.

Tyler, Stephen A. 1969. *Cognitive Anthropology*. N.Y.: Holt, Rinehart and Winston.

Weinreich, Uriel. 1966. "Explorations in semantic theory." In Thomas A. Sebeok (ed.), *Current Trends in Linguistics*, vol. 3. The Hague: Mouton.

Wordick, Frank J.F. 1975. "Sirionô kinship terminology." *International Journal of American Linguistics* 41:242-85.

AFROASIATIC DIALECTS

Afroasiatic Dialects (*AAD*) seeks to provide concise descriptions of individual languages which belong to the Afroasiatic language family. It is primarily directed toward an audience consisting, on the one hand, of students of one or several Afroasiatic languages, and, on the other, of students of linguistics. In these volumes, both these groups should find succinct treatises such as to provide familiarity with the basic structure of the language in question in a comparative perspective. Each description will be comprehensive in scope and sufficiently detailed in exemplification. But at the same time the aim will be to cut through to the essential and to avoid specialized argumentation. The goal then is neither to publish a corpus of exhaustive reference grammars nor to provide a platform for the analytical defense of theoretical questions. In this sense the series is properly data-oriented. Though the authors will necessarily be of a variety of theoretical persuasions and each will have his own set of preferences for presentation, not the least important goal will be to achieve as high a degree as possible of uniformity in structure, and in the conventional signs and terminology used. This being accomplished, the reader should have no difficulty in finding points of resemblance and divergence amongst the languages which concern him with regard to some point of inquiry. The term 'dialects' in the series' title refers not only to modern spoken vernaculars but to historically definable stages of any language of the various branches. Publication of studies of as many such dialects as possible would provide, we feel, both an encouragement to comparative work and a sound documentary base on which alone this work may fruitfully progress.

AAD 1 - **Berber:** *TAMAZIGHT OF THE AYT NDHIR* by Thomas G. Penchoen. 1973, IV-124 pp., $8.50.

The Ayt Ndhir dialect which is described belongs to one of the major Berber languages, Tamazight, spoken in the Middle Atlas Mountains of central Morocco. The description is based in the main on research undertaken with native speakers of the Ayt Ndhir territory surrounding El Hajeb. – While directed to the non-specialist, a number of points in the description proper will be of interest to the specialist as well: the presentation of noun and verb morphology points up a number of regularities which more often than not have been obscured in previous descriptions. Also, phonological rules are given which account for the major share of morphophonemic complexities. The reader will find in the appendices and 'optional' sections conjugation tables of typical verbs–including detailed observations on the placement of shwa in verbs–, a chart showing the main morphological patterns involved in verb derivation, a description of the phonological rules applying in complex sequences of morphemes of the verb group, the 'basic' vocabulary contained in several well-known lexicostatistic word lists, and a chart of the Tifinaγ alphabet used by the Tuareg.

AAD 2 - **Ancient Egyptian:** *MIDDLE EGYPTIAN* by John Callender. 1975, 150 pp., $10.

This grammar deals with the literary language used in Egypt from ca. 2000 to 1200 B.C. and considered in even later times to be the classical written form of Egyptian. The book is directed toward the general linguist as well as the Egyptologist; examples are glossed and written in transcription and there is an index of grammatical terms and Egyptian morphemes. A comprehensive set of paradigms of both verbal and non-verbal predicate types is included as an appendix, together with an appendix on negation and one on the historical origin of certain constructions. – The grammar contains three main parts: phonology, morphology, and syntax, of which the last receives most emphasis. The section on phonology sketches the laws of sound change to the extent they can be discovered. The section on morphology stresses the paradigmatic character of verb tenses and their derivations. A distinction is made between truly paradigmatic tenses and tenses borrowed from Old Egyptian for quotations or special effect. Following Polotsky, the "emphatic forms" are treated as nominalizations under the rubric "manner nominalizations." Unlike previous grammars of Egyptian, this grammar discusses syntax according to transformational categories. The process of "clefting" interrelates emphatic forms, the "participial statement" and constructions with *pw+* relatives. The process character of negation is emphasized, and the implications of so considering it are developed in a special appendix. A sample text is also included, accompanied by a vocabulary and a translation.

AAD 3 - **Semitic:** *DAMASCUS ARABIC* by Arne Ambros. 1977, vii-123 pp., $13.

Based on both previous works and the author's own observations, the grammar describes the Sedentary Eastern Arabic dialect spoken in Damascus. While strictly synchronic and written without presupposing knowledge of classical Arabic, it follows traditional arrangement and terminology as closely as possible without failing however to do justice to the individual traits of the dialect. Appendices deal with 1) the regular reflexes of Classical Arabic phonemes in Damascus Arabic, and rules governing the reduction of vowels, and 2) a discussion of morphological substitutions which cannot be interpreted as describing the historical development from Classical Arabic to Damascus Arabic.
